Sarah, Plain and Tall

PATRICIA MacLACHLAN

For old friends, dear friends—

DICK AND WENDY PUFF,

ALLISON AND DEREK

1

"Did Mama sing every day?" asked Caleb. "Every-single-day?" He sat close to the fire, his **chin** in his hand. It was **dusk**, and the dogs **lay** beside him on the warm **hearthstone**s.

"Every-single-day," I told him for the second time this week. For the twentieth time this month. The hundredth time this year? And the past few years?

"And did Papa sing, too?"

"Yes. Papa sang, too. Don't get so close, Caleb. You'll **heat up**."

He pushed his chair back. It made a **hollow scraping** sound on the hearthstones, and the dogs **stir**red. Lottie, small and black, **wagged** her tail and **lift**ed her head. Nick slept on.

I turned the bread **dough over and over** on the **marble slab** on the kitchen table.

"Well, Papa doesn't sing anymore," said Caleb very softly. A **log** broke apart and **crackled** in the **fireplace**. He looked up at me. "What did I look like when I was born?"

"You didn't have any clothes on," I told him.

"I know that," he said.

"You looked like this." I held the bread dough up in a round **pale** ball.

"I had hair," said Caleb **serious**ly.

"Not enough to talk about," I said.

"And she **name**d me Caleb," he **went on**, **filling** in the old **familiar** story.

"I would have named you **Troublesome**," I said, making Caleb smile.

"And Mama **hand**ed me to you in the yellow **blanket** and said . . ." He waited for me to finish the story. "And said . . . ?"

I **sigh**ed. "And Mama said, 'Isn't he beautiful, Anna?'"

"And I was," Caleb finished.

Caleb thought the story was over, and I didn't tell him what I had really thought. He was **homely** and **plain**, and he had a **terrible holler** and a **horrid** smell. But these were not the worst of him. Mama died the next morning. That was the worst thing about Caleb.

"Isn't he beautiful, Anna?" Her last words to me. I had gone to bed thinking how **wretched** he looked. And I forgot to say good night.

I **wipe**d my hands on my **apron** and went to the window. Outside, the **prairie reach**ed out and touched the places where the sky came down. Though winter was nearly over, there were **patch**es of snow and ice everywhere. I looked at the long **dirt** road that **crawl**ed across the plains,* remembering the morning that Mama had died, **cruel** and sunny. They had come for her in a **wagon** and taken her away to be **buried**. And then the **cousin**s and **aunt**s and **uncle**s had come and tried to fill up the house. But they couldn't.

Slowly, **one by one**, they left. And then the days

---

* plain plain은 책 제목에 쓰인 것처럼 형용사로 '평범한, 수수한, 꾸밈없는'이라는 뜻 외에도 여기서처럼 같은 스펠링의 명사로 '평야, 평지'라는 의미도 가지고 있다. 이 책 전체에 걸쳐서 두 가지 의미가 번갈아 사용되므로 기억해두도록 하자.

seemed long and dark like winter days, even though it wasn't winter. And Papa didn't sing.

Isn't he beautiful, Anna?

No, Mama.

It was hard to think of Caleb as beautiful. It took three **whole** days for me to love him, sitting in the chair by the fire, Papa washing up the **supper** dishes, Caleb's **tiny** hand **brush**ing my cheek. And a smile. It was the smile, I know.

"Can you remember her songs?" asked Caleb. "Mama's songs?"

I turned from the window. "No. Only that she sang about flowers and birds. Sometimes about the moon at nighttime."

Caleb reached down and touched Lottie's head.

"Maybe," he said, his voice low, "if you remember the songs, then I might remember her, too."

My eyes **widen**ed and tears came. Then the door opened and wind **blew** in with Papa, and I went to stir the **stew**. Papa put his arms around me and put his nose in my hair.

"Nice **soapy** smell, that stew," he said.

I laughed. "That's my hair."

Caleb came over and **threw** his arms around Papa's neck and **hung** down as Papa **swung** him **back and forth,** and the dogs sat up.

"Cold in town," said Papa. "And Jack was **feisty.**" Jack was Papa's horse that he'd **raised** from a **colt.** "**Rascal,**" **murmur**ed Papa, smiling, because no matter what Jack did Papa loved him.

I **spoon**ed up the stew and lighted the oil lamp and we ate with the dogs **crowd**ing under the table, hoping for **spills** or **handout**s.

Papa might not have told us about Sarah that night if Caleb hadn't asked him the question. After the dishes were cleared and washed and Papa was filling the **tin pail** with **ash**es, Caleb spoke up. It wasn't a question, really.

"You don't sing anymore," he said. He said it **harsh**ly. Not because he **mean**t to, but because he had been thinking of it for so long. "Why?" he asked more **gently.**

Slowly Papa **straighten**ed up. There was a long **silence,** and the dogs looked up, wondering at it.

"I've forgotten the old songs," said Papa quietly. He sat down. "But maybe there's a way to remember them."

He looked up at us.

"How?" asked Caleb **eagerly**.

Papa **lean**ed back in the chair. "I've **placed an advertisement** in the newspapers. For help."

"You mean a **housekeeper**?" I asked, surprised.

Caleb and I looked at each other and **burst** out laughing, remembering Hilly, our old housekeeper. She was round and slow and **shuffling**. She **snore**d in a high **whistle** at night, like a tea**kettle**, and let the fire go out.

"No," said Papa slowly. "Not a housekeeper." He **paused**. "A wife."

Caleb **stare**d at Papa. "A wife? You mean a Mother? "

Nick **slid** his face onto Papa's **lap** and Papa **stroked** his ears.

"That, too," said Papa. "Like Maggie."

Matthew, our neighbor to the south, had written to ask for a wife and mother for his children. And Maggie had come from Tennessee.* Her hair was the color of **turnips** and she laughed.

Papa reached into his pocket and **unfold**ed a letter

---

* Tennessee 테네시 주. 미국 남동부에 위치해 있으며, 주변 8개 주에 둘러싸여 있는 내륙에 위치한 주이다.

written on white paper. "And I have **received** an answer."
Papa read to us:

"Dear Mr. Jacob Witting,

I am Sarah Wheaten from Maine* as you will see
from my letter. I am answering your advertisement. I
have never been married, though I have been asked.
I have lived with an older brother, William, who is
about to be married. His wife-to-be is young and
energetic.

I have always loved to live by the sea, but at this
time I feel a move is necessary. And the truth is, the
sea is as far east as I can go. My choice, as you can
see, is **limited**.* This should not be taken as an **insult**.
I am strong and I work hard and I am willing to travel.
But I am not **mild mannered**. If you should still care
to write, I would be interested in your children and
about where you live. And you.

Very truly yours,

＊Maine 메인 주. 미국의 북동쪽 가장 끝, 바다와 접한 지점에 위치해 있다.
＊My choice, as you can see, is limited Maine주가 미국 동쪽 가장 끝에 위치해 있기
때문에 이렇게 말한 것이다(as far east as I can go). 지리적 위치 상 더 이상 동쪽으로 갈 수도
없고 Anna네 가족이 살고 있는 서부 지역으로 가야하는 상황이라고 위트 있게 말하고 있다.

Sarah Elisabeth Wheaten

P.S. Do you have **opinions** on cats? I have one."

No one spoke when Papa finished the letter. He kept looking at it in his hands, reading it over to himself. Finally I turned my head a **bit** to **sneak** a look at Caleb. He was smiling. I smiled, too.

"One thing," I said in the quiet of the room.

"What's that?" asked Papa, looking up.

I put my arm around Caleb.

"Ask her if she sings," I said.

2

Caleb and Papa and I wrote letters to Sarah, and before the ice and snow had **melt**ed from the fields, we all **receive**d answers. Mine came first.

Dear Anna,

Yes, I can **braid** hair and I can make **stew** and **bake** bread, though I **prefer** to build **bookshelves** and paint.

My **favorite** colors are the colors of the sea, blue and gray and green, depending on the weather. My brother William is a fisherman, and he tells me that when he is in the middle of a **fog-bound** sea the water is a color for which there is no name. He catches flounder and sea bass and bluefish.[*] Sometimes he sees **whale**s. And birds, too, of course. I am **enclosing** a book of sea birds so you will see what William and I see every day.

Very truly yours,
Sarah Elisabeth Wheaten

Caleb read and read the letter so many times that the ink began to run and the **folds tore**. He read the book about sea birds **over and over**.

"Do you think she'll come?" asked Caleb. "And will she **stay**? What if she thinks we are loud and **pesky**?"

"You *are* loud and pesky," I told him. But I was worried, too. Sarah loved the sea, I could tell. Maybe she wouldn't leave there after all to come where there were fields and grass and sky and not much else.

"What if she comes and doesn't like our house?" Caleb asked. "I told her it was small. Maybe I shouldn't have

---

＊ flounder, sea bass, bluefish 모두 바닷물고기 명칭이다. flounder는 가자밋과의 물고기의 총칭으로 주로 넓적한 몸통에 한쪽으로 눈이 몰려서 달려 있다. sea bass는 '농어'로 몸이 가늘고 길며 등은 회청록색, 배는 은백색을 띄고 있는 우리나라에서도 흔히 볼 수 있는 물고기이다. bluefish 역시 농어목 게르칫과의 바닷물고기이다.

14

told her it was small."

"**Hush**, Caleb. Hush."

Caleb's letter came soon after, with a picture of a cat **draw**n on the **envelope**.

Dear Caleb,

My cat's name is Seal because she is gray like the **seal**s that swim **offshore** in Maine. She is glad that Lottie and Nick send their greetings. She likes dogs most of the time. She says their **footprint**s are much larger than hers (which she is enclosing in return).

Your house sounds lovely, even though it is far out in the country with no close neighbors. My house is tall and the **shingle**s are gray because of the **salt** from the sea. There are roses **nearby**.

Yes, I do like small rooms sometimes. Yes, I can keep a fire going at night. I do not know if I **snore**. Seal has never told me.

Very truly yours,
Sarah Elisabeth

"Did you really ask her about fires and snoring?" I

asked, **amazed**.

"I wished to know," Caleb said.

He kept the letter with him, reading it in the **barn** and in the fields and by the cow **pond**. And always in bed at night.

One morning, early, Papa and Caleb and I were cleaning out the horse **stalls** and putting down new **bedding**. Papa stopped suddenly and **lean**ed on his **pitchfork**.

"Sarah has said she will come for a month's time if we wish her to," he said, his voice loud in the dark barn. "To see how it is. Just to see."

Caleb stood by the stall door and **fold**ed his **arms** across his **chest**.

"I think," he began. Then, "I think," he said slowly, "that it would be good—to say yes," he finished **in a rush**.

Papa looked at me.

"I say yes," I told him, **grin**ning.

"Yes," said Papa. "Then yes it is."

And the three of us, all smiling, went to work again.

The next day Papa went to town to mail his letter to Sarah. It was rainy for days, and the clouds **followed**.

The house was cool and **damp** and quiet. Once I set four places at the table, then caught myself and put the **extra** plate away. Three **lamb**s were born, one with a black face. And then Papa's letter came. It was very short.

Dear Jacob,

I will come by train. I will wear a yellow **bonnet**. I am **plain** and tall.

Sarah

"What's that?" asked Caleb excitedly, **peer**ing over Papa's shoulder. He pointed. "There, written at the bottom of the letter."

Papa read it to himself. Then he smiled, holding up the letter for us to see.

Tell them I sing was all it said.

3

Sarah came in the spring. She came through green grass fields that **bloom**ed with Indian paintbrush,* red and orange, and blue-eyed grass.

Papa got up early for the long day's trip to the train and back. He **brush**ed his hair so **slick** and **shiny** that Caleb laughed. He wore a clean blue shirt, and a belt instead of **suspenders**.

---

* Indian paintbrush 인디언붓꽃. 아메리카 지역에 서식하는 다년생 꽃으로 주로 붉은 색을 띄고 있다. 꽃의 명칭은 한 전설에서 유래했다고 하는데 그 내용을 간략히 소개하면 다음과 같다. 옛날 한 인디언 청년이 저녁노을을 그리고 있었다. 하지만 불타는 노을 색을 찾을 길이 없어 '위대한 영(Great Spirit)'에게 도움을 청했고, 이 위대한 영은 청년이 원하던 색을 붓에 묻혀주어 걸작을 만들 수 있도록 도와주었다. 인디언 청년은 그림을 완성하고는 그 붓을 들판에 버렸는데, 이 붓이 싹터 핀 꽃이 바로 '인디언붓꽃'이다.

He **fed** and **water**ed the horses, talking to them as he **hitch**ed them up to the wagon. Old Bess, calm and kind; Jack, wild-eyed, **reach**ing over to **nip** Bess on the neck.

"Clear day, Bess," said Papa, **rub**bing her nose.

"**Settle** down, Jack." He **lean**ed his head on Jack.

And then Papa **drove off** along the **dirt** road to **fetch** Sarah. Papa's new wife. Maybe. Maybe our new mother.

Gophers* ran **back and forth** across the road, stopping to stand up and watch the wagon. **Far off** in a field a woodchuck* ate and listened. Ate and listened.

Caleb and I did our **chores** without talking. We **shovel**ed out the **stalls** and **laid** down new **hay.*** We fed the **sheep**. We **swept** and **straighten**ed and carried wood and water. And then our chores were done.

Caleb pulled on my shirt.

"Is my face clean?" he asked. "Can my face be *too* clean?" He looked **alarmed**.

---

* gopher 땅다람쥐. 땅속 굴에 사는 쥐같이 생긴 북아메리카에 서식하는 동물.
* woodchuck 마멋 혹은 마모트라고 불리는 북아메리카산 다람쥣과의 설치류 동물.
* laid down new hay 이 문장에서 쓰인 동사 lay(~을 놓다, 두다)는 앞서 나왔던 lie(눕다, 누워 있다)와 의미도 유사하고 과거형 스펠링도 비슷해서 혼동하기 쉬우니 주의하도록 하자. 이 문장에서 '새로운 건초(new hay)를' 내려놓았다(laid down)라고 쓰인 것처럼, lay는 '행동의 대상'이 따라와야 하는 동사(타동사)이며, 동사 변화는 lay—laid—laid, laying이다. 반면 lie는 의미는 유사하나 주어가 스스로 동작할 뿐 행동의 대상이 필요 없는 동사(자동사)이고, 동사 변화는 lie—lay—lain, lying이다.

"No, your face is clean but not too clean," I said.

Caleb **slip**ped his hand into mine as we stood on the **porch**, watching the road. He was afraid.

"Will she be nice?" he asked. "Like Maggie?"

"Sarah will be nice," I told him.

"How far away is Maine?" he asked.

"You know how far. Far away, by the sea."

"Will Sarah bring some sea?" he asked.

"No, you cannot bring the sea."

The sheep ran in the field, and far off the cows moved slowly to the **pond**, like **turtle**s.

"Will she like us?" asked Caleb very softly.

I watched a marsh **hawk**[*] **wheel** down behind the **barn**.

He looked up at me.

"Of course she will like us." He answered his own question. "We are nice," he added, making me smile.

We waited and watched. I **rock**ed on the porch and Caleb **roll**ed a **marble** on the wood floor. Back and forth.

---

* marsh hawk 회색개구리매. 매(hawk)의 한 종류로 저지대 습지나 물가 또는 갈대밭에 살면서 물고기 · 뱀 · 개구리 · 물새 따위를 잡아먹는다. marsh는 '습지'라는 의미인데, 주로 습지 근처에서 서식하며 먹이를 잡기 때문에 이런 이름이 붙었다.

Back and forth. The marble was blue.

We saw the **dust** from the **wagon** first, rising above the road, above the heads of Jack and Old Bess. Caleb **climb**ed up onto the porch **roof** and **shade**d his eyes.

"A bonnet!" he cried. "I see a yellow bonnet!"

The dogs came out from under the porch, ears up, their eyes on the cloud of dust bringing Sarah. The wagon **pass**ed the **fenced** field, and the cows and sheep looked up, too. It rounded the **windmill** and the barn and the **windbreak** of Russian olive* that Mama had **plant**ed long ago. Nick began to **bark**, then Lottie, and the wagon **clatter**ed into the yard and stopped by the steps.

"**Hush**," said Papa to the dogs.

And it was quiet.

Sarah stepped down from the wagon, a cloth bag in her hand. She reached up and **took off** her yellow bonnet, **smooth**ing back her brown hair into a **bun**. She was **plain** and tall.

"Did you bring some sea?" cried Caleb beside me.

"Something from the sea," said Sarah, smiling. "And

＊Russian olive 보리수나무. 높이 5~7미터 정도의 낙엽활엽수로 가을 즈음에 먹을 수 있는 열매가 열린다.

me." She turned and **lifted** a black case from the wagon. "And Seal, too."

Carefully she opened the case, and Seal, gray with white feet, stepped out. Lottie **lay** down, her head on her **paws**, **staring**. Nick leaned down to **sniff**. Then he lay down, too.

"The cat will be good in the barn," said Papa. "For **mice**."

Sarah smiled. "She will be good in the house, too."

Sarah took Caleb's hand, then mine. Her hands were large and **rough**. She gave Caleb a **shell**—a moon **snail**,[*] she called it—that was **curl**ed and smelled of **salt**.

"The **gull**s fly high and drop the shells on the rocks below," she told Caleb. "When the shell is broken, they eat what is inside."

"That is very smart," said Caleb.

"For you, Anna," said Sarah, "a sea stone."

And she gave me the smoothest and whitest stone I had ever seen.

"The sea washes **over and over** and around the stone,

✷ moon snail 구슬우렁이. 바다 우렁이(sea snail)의 한 종류.

rolling it until it is round and perfect."

"That is very smart, too," said Caleb. He looked up at Sarah. "We do not have the sea here."

Sarah turned and looked out over the plains.

"No," she said. "There is no sea here. But the land rolls a little like the sea."

My father did not see her look, but I did. And I knew that Caleb had seen it, too. Sarah was not smiling. Sarah was already **lonely**. In a month's time the **preacher** might come to marry Sarah and Papa. And a month was a long time. Time enough for her to change her mind and leave us.

Papa took Sarah's bags inside, where her room was ready with a **quilt** on the bed and blue flax* **dried** in a **vase** on the night table.

Seal **stretch**ed and made a small cat sound. I watched her **circle** the dogs and sniff the air. Caleb came out and stood beside me.

"When will we sing?" he **whisper**ed.

I **shook** my head, turning the white stone over and

＊blue flax 아마(亞麻)꽃. 아마는 중앙아시아 원산의 한해살이풀로 파란빛을 띤 꽃이 피며 그 껍질이 섬유를 만드는 데 사용되기도 한다.

over in my hand. I wished everything was as perfect as the stone. I wished that Papa and Caleb and I were perfect for Sarah. I wished we had a sea of our own.

4

The dogs loved Sarah first. Lottie slept beside her bed, curled in a soft circle, and Nick leaned his face on the covers in the morning, watching for the first sign that Sarah was awake. No one knew where Seal slept. Seal was a roamer.

Sarah's collection of shells sat on the windowsill.

"A scallop," she told us, picking up the shells one by one, "a sea clam, an oyster, a razor clam. And a conch shell.* If you put it to your ear you can hear the sea." She

---

* scallop, sea clam, oyster, razor clam, conch shell 모두 조개류의 이름이다. scallop 은 '가리비', sea clam은 '대합조개', oyster는 '굴', razor clam은 '맛조개', conch shell은 '소라'이 다.

put it to Caleb's ear, then mine. Papa listened, too. Then Sarah listened once more, with a look so sad and far away that Caleb leaned against me.

"**At least** Sarah can hear the sea," he **whispere**d.

Papa was quiet and **shy** with Sarah, and so was I. But Caleb talked to Sarah from morning until the light left the sky.

"Where are you going?" he asked. "To do what?"

"To pick flowers," said Sarah. "I'll **hang** some of them **upside down** and **dry** them so they'll keep some color. And we can have flowers all winter long."

"I'll come, too!" cried Caleb. "Sarah said winter," he said to me. "That **means** Sarah will stay."

Together we picked flowers, paintbrush and clover and **prairie** violets. * There were **bud**s on the wild roses that **climb**ed up the **paddock fence**.

"The roses will **bloom** in early summer," I told Sarah. I looked to see if she knew what I was thinking. Summer was when the **wedding** would be. *Might* be. Sarah and Papa's wedding.

★ paintbrush, clover, prairie violet 모두 들판에 피는 꽃 이름이다. paintbrush는 앞서 설명한 인디언붓꽃, clover는 토끼풀꽃, prairie violet는 제비꽃이다.

We hung the flowers from the **ceiling** in little **bunch**es. "I've never seen this before," said Sarah. "What is it called?"

"**Bride's bonnet**," I told her.

Caleb smiled at the name.

"We don't have this by the sea," she said. "We have **seaside** goldenrod and wild asters and **woolly** ragwort.*"

"Woolly ragwort!" Caleb **whoop**ed. He **made up** a song.

"Woolly ragwort all around,

Woolly ragwort on the ground.

Woolly ragwort grows and grows,

Woolly ragwort in your nose."

Sarah and Papa laughed, and the dogs **lift**ed their heads and **thump**ed their tails against the wood floor. Seal sat on a kitchen chair and watched us with yellow eyes.

＊ goldenrod, aster, woolly ragwort 모두 식물 이름이다. goldenrod는 '미역취'라는 풀로 노란색 꽃이 피며, aster는 '개미취'라는 풀로 연한 자주색 꽃이 핀다. woolly ragwort는 '털머위'라는 풀로 암꽃은 백색, 수꽃은 황백색 꽃이 핀다.

We ate Sarah's **stew**, the late light coming through the windows. Papa had **baked** bread that was still warm from the fire.

"The stew is fine," said Papa.

"Ayuh." Sarah **nod**ded. "The bread, too."

"What does 'ayuh' mean?" asked Caleb.

"In Maine it means yes," said Sarah. "Do you want more stew?"

"Ayuh," said Caleb.

"Ayuh," **echo**ed my father.

After dinner Sarah told us about William. "He has a gray-and-white boat **named** *Kittiwake*." She looked out the window. "That is a small **gull** found way **off the shore** where William **fish**es. There are three **aunts** who live near us. They wear **silk** dresses and no shoes. You would love them."

"Ayuh," said Caleb.

"Does your brother look like you?" I asked.

"Yes," said Sarah. "He is **plain** and tall."

At **dusk** Sarah cut Caleb's hair on the front steps, **gather**ing his curls and **scatter**ing them on the fence and ground. Seal **bat**ted some hair around the **porch** as the dogs watched.

"Why?" asked Caleb.

"For the birds," said Sarah. "They will use it for their **nest**s. Later we can look for nests of curls."

"Sarah said 'later,'" Caleb whispered to me as we **spread** his hair about. "Sarah will **stay**."

Sarah cut Papa's hair, too. No one else saw, but I found him behind the barn, **toss**ing the pieces of hair into the wind for the birds.

Sarah **brush**ed my hair and **tied** it up in back with a rose velvet* ribbon she had brought from Maine. She brushed hers long and free and tied it back, too, and we stood **side by side** looking into the **mirror**. I looked taller, like Sarah, and **fair** and thin. And with my hair pulled back I looked a little like her **daughter**. Sarah's daughter.

And then it was time for singing.

Sarah sang us a song we had never heard before as we sat on the porch, **insects buzz**ing in the dark, the **rustle** of cows in the grasses. It was called "Sumer Is Icumen in,*" and she taught it to us all, even Papa, who sang as if

---

＊ velvet 벨벳, 벨벳으로 만든. 벨벳은 거죽에 곱고 짧은 털이 촘촘히 돋게 짠 비단이다.
＊ Summer Is Icumen in 13세기 영국의 돌림노래 '여름은 오도다(Summer has come in)'. 계절, 자연을 찬미하는 내용이다.

he had never stopped singing.

"*Sumer is icumen in*
Lhude sing cuccu!"

"What is sumer?" asked Caleb. He said it "soomer,"
the way Sarah had said it.

"Summer," said Papa and Sarah at the same time.
Caleb and I looked at each other. Summer was coming.

"Tomorrow," said Sarah, "I want to see the **sheep**. You
know, I've never touched one."

"Never?" Caleb sat up.

"Never," said Sarah. She smiled and leaned back in her
chair. "But I've touched **seal**s. Real seals. They are cool
and **slippery** and they **slide** through the water like fish.
They can cry and sing. And sometimes they **bark**, a little
like dogs."

Sarah barked like a seal. And Lottie and Nick came
running from the barn to jump up on Sarah and **lick**
her face and make her laugh. Sarah **stroke**d them and
scratched their ears and it was quiet again.

"I wish I could touch a seal right now," said Caleb, his

voice soft in the night.

"So do I," said Sarah. She **sigh**ed, then she began to sing the summer song again. **Far off** in a field, a meadowlark* sang, too.

---

* meadowlark 들종다리. 들판이나 목초지(meadow)에 사는 종다리(lark). 종다리는 종달새라고도 불리는 참새와 비슷한 모양의 새이다.

5

The **sheep** made Sarah smile. She **sank** her fingers into their **thick**, **coarse wool**. She talked to them, running with the **lamb**s, letting them **suck** on her fingers. She **name**d them after her **favorite aunt**s, Harriet and Mattie and Lou. She **lay** down in the field beside them and sang "Sumer Is Icumen in," her voice **drift**ing over the **meadow** grasses, carried by the wind.

She cried when we found a lamb that had died, and she shouted and **shook** her **fist** at the turkey buzzards*

---

* turkey buzzard 독수리의 일종. 칠면조(turkey)처럼 붉은 머리를 가진 독수리(buzzard) 로, 자연사한 갓 죽은 짐승의 싱싱한 고기만 먹는다. 이런 습성 때문에 죽음을 상징하는 새 이기도 하다.

that came from **nowhere** to eat it. She would not let Caleb or me come near. And that night, Papa went with a **shovel** to **bury** the sheep and a **lantern** to bring Sarah back. She sat on the **porch alone**. Nick **crept** up to **lean** against her **knee**s.

After dinner, Sarah **drew** pictures to send home to Maine. She began a **charcoal drawing*** of the fields, **roll**ing like the sea rolled. She drew a sheep whose ears were too big. And she drew a **windmill**.

"Windmill was my first word," said Caleb. "Papa told me so."

"Mine was flower," I said. "What was yours, Sarah?"

"**Dune**," said Sarah.

"Dune?" Caleb looked up.

"In Maine," said Sarah, "there are rock **cliff**s that rise up at the **edge** of the sea. And there are hills **cover**ed with **pine** and spruce trees,* green with **needle**s. But William and I found a sand dune all our own. It was soft and **sparkling** with **bits** of mica,* and when we were little

---

* charcoal drawing 목탄화. 목탄으로 그린 단색 그림.
* spruce tree 가문비나무. 소나무과의 나무의 일종으로, 일 년 내내 푸른 잎을 가진 상록수(evergreen)이며 잎이 바늘(needle)같이 뾰족한 침엽수이다.
* mica 운모(雲母). 석영 및 장석과 함께 화강암을 구성하는 중요 광물이다. 운모가 포함되어 있는 바위는 반짝거리기 때문에 '돌비늘'이라고도 불린다.

we would slide down the dune into the water."

Caleb looked out the window.

"We have no dunes here," he said.

Papa stood up.

"Yes we do," he said. He took the lantern and went out the door to the **barn**.

"We do?" Caleb called after him.

He ran ahead, Sarah and I **follow**ing, the dogs close behind.

Next to the barn was Papa's **mound** of **hay** for **bedding**, nearly as tall as the barn, covered with canvas* to keep the rain from **rot**ting it. Papa carried the **wooden ladder** from the barn and leaned it against the hay.

"There." He smiled at Sarah. "Our dune."

Sarah was very quiet. The dogs looked up at her, waiting. Seal **brush**ed against her legs, her tail in the air. Caleb **reach**ed over and took her hand.

"It looks high up," he said. "Are you **scared**, Sarah?"

"Scared? Scared!" **exclaim**ed Sarah. "You **bet** I'm not scared."

＊ canvas 범포(帆布), 캔버스 천. 텐트 · 돛 · 화폭 등을 만드는 데 쓰이는 질긴 천.

She **climb**ed the ladder, and Nick began to **bark**. She climbed to the very top of the hay and sat, looking down at us. Above, the stars were coming out. Papa **piled** a bed of **loose** hay below with his **pitchfork**. The light of the lantern made his eyes shine when he smiled up at Sarah.

"Fine?" called Papa.

"Fine," said Sarah. She **lifted** her arms over her head and **slid** down, down, into the soft hay. She lay, laughing, as the dogs rolled beside her.

"Was it a good dune?" called Caleb.

"Yes," said Sarah. "It is a fine dune."

Caleb and I climbed up and slid down. And Sarah did it three more times. At last Papa slid down, too, as the sky grew darker and the stars **blink**ed like **fireflies**. We were covered with hay and **dust**, and we **sneezed**.

In the kitchen, Caleb and I washed in the big wooden **tub** and Sarah drew more pictures to send to William. One was of Papa, his hair **curly** and full of hay. She drew Caleb, sliding down the hay, his arms like Sarah's over his head. And she drew a picture of me in the tub, my hair long and straight and **wet**. She looked at her drawing of the fields for a long time.

"Something is **miss**ing," she told Caleb. "Something."
And she put it away.

"'Dear William,'" Sarah read to us by lantern light that night. "'Sliding down our dune of hay is almost as fine as sliding down the sand dunes into the sea.'"

Caleb smiled at me across the table. He said nothing, but his mouth **form**ed the words I had heard, too. *Our dune.*

6

The days grew longer. The cows moved close to the **pond**, where the water was cool and there were trees.

Papa taught Sarah how to **plow** the fields, guiding the plow behind Jack and Old Bess, the **rein**s around her neck. When the **chore**s were done we sat in the **meadow** with the **sheep**, Sarah beside us, watching Papa finish.

"Tell me about winter," said Sarah.

Old Bess **nod**ded her head as she walked, but we could hear Papa speak **sharply** to Jack.

"Jack doesn't like work," said Caleb. "He wants to be here in the sweet grass with us."

"I don't **blame** him," said Sarah. She **lay** back in the grass with her arms under her head. "Tell me about winter," she said again.

"Winter is cold here," said Caleb, and Sarah and I laughed.

"Winter is cold everywhere," I said.

"We go to school in winter," said Caleb. "**Sums** and writing and books," he sang.

"I am good at sums and writing," said Sarah. "I love books. How do you get to school?"

"Papa drives us in the **wagon**. Or we walk the three miles when there is not too much snow."

Sarah sat up. "Do you have lots of snow?"

"Lots and lots and lots of snow," **chant**ed Caleb, **roll**ing around in the grass. "Sometimes we have to **dig** our way out to **feed** the animals."

"In Maine the **barns** are **attach**ed to the houses sometimes," said Sarah.

Caleb **grin**ned. "So you could have a cow to Sunday **supper**?"

Sarah and I laughed.

"When there are bad **storms**, Papa **ties** a **rope** from the house to the barn so no one will get **lost**," said Caleb.

I **frown**ed. I loved winter.

"There is ice on the windows on winter mornings," I told Sarah. "We can **draw sparkling** pictures and we can see our **breath** in the air. Papa builds a warm fire, and we **bake** hot **biscuit**s and put on hundreds of **sweater**s. And if the snow is too high, we **stay** home from school and make **snow people**."

Sarah lay back in the tall grasses again, her face nearly **hidden**.

"And is there wind?" she asked.

"Do you like wind?" asked Caleb.

"There is wind by the sea," said Sarah.

"There is wind here," said Caleb happily. "It blows the snow and brings tumbleweeds* and makes the sheep run. Wind and wind and wind!" Caleb stood up and ran like the wind, and the sheep ran after him. Sarah and I watched him jump over rock and **gullies**, the sheep behind him, **stiff legged** and fast. He **circle**d the field, the sun making the top of his hair golden. He **collapse**d next to Sarah,

---

* tumbleweed 회전초. 가을이 되면 줄기 밑동에서 떨어져 공 모양으로 바람에 날리는 잡초. 바람에 날려 굴러다니는(tumble) 잡초(weed)이기 때문에 이런 이름이 붙여졌다.

and the **lamb**s pushed their **wet** noses into us.

"Hello, Lou," said Sarah, smiling. "Hello, Mattie."

The sun rose higher, and Papa stopped to take off his hat and **wipe** his face with his **sleeve**.

"I'm hot," said Sarah. "I can't wait for winter wind. Let's swim."

"Swim where?" I asked her.

"I can't swim," said Caleb.

"Can't swim!" **exclaim**ed Sarah. "I'll teach you in the cow pond."

"That's for cows!" I cried.

But Sarah had **grab**bed our hands and we were running through the fields, **duck**ing under the **fence** to the far pond.

"**Shoo**, cows," said Sarah as the cows looked up, **startle**d. She **took off** her dress and **wade**d into the water in her petticoat.* She **dive**d suddenly and **disappear**ed for a moment as Caleb and I watched. She came up, laughing, her hair **stream**ing free. Water **bead**s sat on her shoulders.

She tried to teach us how to **float**. I **sank** like a **bucket**

---

*petticoat 치마 안쪽에 속옷처럼 입는 여성용 속치마.

filled with water and came up **sputter**ing. But Caleb lay on his back and learned how to **blow** streams of water high in the air like a **whale**. The cows stood on the **banks** of the pond and **stare**d and stopped their **chew**ing. Water **bug**s circled us.

"Is this like the sea?" asked Caleb.

Sarah **tread**ed water.

"The sea is **salt**," said Sarah. "It **stretch**es out as far as you can see. It **gleam**s like the sun on glass. There are **wave**s."

"Like this?" asked Caleb, and he pushed a wave at Sarah, making her **cough** and laugh.

"Yes," she said. "Like that."

I held my breath and floated at last, looking up into the sky, afraid to speak. **Crow**s flew over, three in a **row**. And I could hear a killdeer* in the field.

We **climb**ed the bank and **dried** ourselves and lay in the grass again. The cows watched, their eyes sad in their dinner-plate* faces. And I slept, dreaming a perfect

---

＊ killdeer 물떼새의 일종. 새가 지저귀는 소리가 kill-dee처럼 들리기 때문에 이런 이름이 붙여졌다고 한다.
＊ dinner-plate 정찬용 접시. 주요한 음식을 담는 접시. 혹은 그 접시처럼 '크고 평평한 모양을 가진'.

dream. The fields had turned to a sea that gleamed like sun on glass. And Sarah was happy.

7

The dandelions* in the fields had gone by, their heads
soft as **feather**s. The summer roses were opening.

Our neighbors, Matthew and Maggie, came to help
Papa **plow** up a new field for corn. Sarah stood with us on
the **porch**, watching their **wagon wind** up the road,* two
horses pulling it and one **tie**d in back. I remembered the
last time we had stood here **alone**, Caleb and I, waiting
for Sarah.

---

* dandelion 민들레. 꽃이 지고 나면 그 자리에 흰 털을 가진 씨앗이 붙는다.
* wind up the road 이 문장에서 쓰인 wind는 동사로 '구불구불하다, 구불구불하게 굽이
치며 길을 오다(wind up)'는 의미로 쓰였다. 바람을 의미하는 wind와 발음과 의미 모두 다
르니 주의하자.

Sarah's hair was in **thick braid**s that **circle**d her head, wild daisies⃰ **tucke**d here and there. Papa had picked them for her.

Old Bess and Jack ran along the inside of the **fence**, **whicke**ring at the new horses.

"Papa needs five horses for the big **gang** plow⃰," Caleb told Sarah. "**Prairie** grass is hard."

Matthew and Maggie came with their two children and a **sackful** of chickens. Maggie **emptie**d the **sack** into the yard and three red **banty** chickens **cluck**ed and **scatter**ed.

"They are for you," she told Sarah. "For eating."

Sarah loved the chickens. She clucked back to them and **fed** them **grain**. They **followed** her, **shuffling** and **scratch**ing **primly** in the **dirt**. I knew they would not be for eating.

The children were young and **name**d Rose and Violet, after flowers. They **hoot**ed and laughed and **chased** the chickens, who flew up to the porch **roof**, then the dogs, who **crept** quietly under the porch. Seal had long ago

⃰ daisy 데이지 꽃.
⃰ gang plow 복식 쟁기. 넓은 면적을 한꺼번에 경작하기 위해 여러 쟁기(plow)를 무리 (gang)지어 이어 붙인 것

fled to the barn to sleep in cool **hay**.

Sarah and Maggie helped **hitch** the horses to the plow, then they set up a big table in the **shade** of the barn, **cover**ing it with a **quilt** and a **kettle** of flowers in the middle. They sat on the porch while Caleb and Matthew and Papa began their morning of plowing. I mixed biscuit **dough** just inside the door, watching.

"You are **lonely**, yes?" asked Maggie in her soft voice.

Sarah's eyes **filled** with tears. Slowly I **stir**red the dough.

Maggie **reach**ed over and took Sarah's hand. "I **miss** the hills of Tennessee sometimes," she said.

Do not miss the hills, Maggie, I thought.

"I miss the sea," said Sarah.

Do not miss the hills. Do not miss the sea.

I stirred and stirred the dough.

"I miss my brother William," said Sarah. "But he is married. The house is hers now. Not mine any longer. There are three old **aunts** who all **squawk** together like **crow**s at **dawn**. I miss them, too."

"There are always things to miss," said Maggie. "No matter where you are."

I looked out and saw Papa and Matthew and Caleb working. Rose and Violet ran in the fields. I felt something **brush** my legs and looked down at Nick, **wagging** his tail.

"I would miss you, Nick," I **whisper**ed. "I would." I **knelt** down and scratched his ears. "I miss Mama."

"I nearly forgot," said Maggie on the porch. "I have something more for you."

I carried the **bowl** outside and watched Maggie **lift** a low wooden box out of the wagon.

"**Plant**s," she said to Sarah. "For your garden."

"My garden?" Sarah **bent** down to touch the plants.

"Zinnias and marigolds and wild feverfew,*" said Maggie. "You must have a garden. Wherever you are."

Sarah smiled. "I had a garden in Maine with dahlias and columbine. And nasturtiums the color of the sun when it sets. I don't know if nasturtiums would grow here."

★ zinnia, marigold, feverfew zinnia, marigold, feverfew와 아래에 계속 이어져 나오는 dahlia, columbine, nasturtium 그리고 tansy는 모두 식물 이름이다. 따로 암기할 필요 없이 참고해두기만 하자. zinnia의 한글 명칭은 '백일홍'으로 꽃이 100일 동안 붉게 핀다는 의미 이다. marigold는 '금송화, 금잔화, 만수국' 등의 다양한 이름으로 불리는 관상용 꽃으로 잔 물결이 잡혀진 모양의 화려한 색상을 가지고 있다. feverfew는 초롱꽃목 국화과의 여러해 살이풀로 '화란국화'라고도 불린다. 열(fever)을 내리는 치료 효과를 가지고 있는데서 이름 이 유래했다. dahlia도 역시 초롱꽃목 국화과의 여러해살이풀로 관상용으로 많이 심는다. columbine은 '매발톱꽃'으로 꽃잎 뒤쪽에 '꽃뿔'이라고 하는 꿀주머니가 있는데, 매의 발톱 처럼 안으로 굽은 모양이어서 이런 이름이 붙여졌다. nasturtium은 '한련화'로 남아메리카 가 주 원산지인 여러해살이풀이다. (이후 마지막 챕터에도 한번 더 등장한다.)

"Try," said Maggie. "You must have a garden."

We planted the flowers by the porch, turning over the **soil** and **pat**ting it around them, and **water**ing. Lottie and Nick came to **sniff**, and the chickens walked in the dirt, leaving **print**s. In the fields, the horses pulled the plow up and down under the hot summer sun.

Maggie **wipe**d her face, leaving a **streak** of dirt.

"Soon you can drive your wagon over to my house and I will give you more. I have tansy.*"

Sarah **frown**ed. "I have never driven a wagon."

"I can teach you," said Maggie. "And so can Anna and Caleb. And Jacob."

Sarah turned to me. "Can you?" she asked. "Can you drive a wagon? "

I **nod**ded.

"And Caleb?"

"Yes."

"In Maine," said Sarah, "I would walk to town."

"Here it is different," said Maggie. "Here you will drive."

---

* tansy 앞서 나온 식물들과 마찬가지로 초롱꽃목 국화과의 여러해살이풀이로 한글 명칭은 '쑥국화'이다.

Way off in the sky, clouds **gather**ed. Matthew and Papa and Caleb came in from the fields, their work done. We all ate in the shade.

"We are glad you are here," said Matthew to Sarah. "A new friend. Maggie misses her friends sometimes."

Sarah nodded. "There is always something to miss, no matter where you are," she said, smiling at Maggie.

Rose and Violet **fell asleep** in the grass, their **bellies** full of meat and **greens** and biscuits. And when it was time to go, Papa and Matthew lifted them into the wagon to sleep on **blanket**s.

Sarah walked slowly behind the wagon for a long time, **waving**, watching it **disappear**. Caleb and I ran to bring her back, the chickens running wildly behind us.

"What shall we name them?" asked Sarah, laughing as the chickens followed us into the house.

I smiled. I was right. The chickens would not be for eating.

And then Papa came, just before the rain, bringing Sarah the first roses of summer.

8

The rain came and **pass**ed, but **strange** clouds **hung** in the northwest, low and black and green. And the air grew still.

In the morning, Sarah dressed in a pair of **overall**s and went to the **barn** to have an **argument** with Papa. She took apples for Old Bess and Jack.

"Women don't wear overalls," said Caleb, running along behind her like one of Sarah's chickens.

"This woman does," said Sarah **crisp**ly.

Papa stood by the **fence**.

"I want to learn how to **ride** a horse," Sarah told him.

"And then I want to learn how to drive the **wagon. By myself**."

Jack **lean**ed over and **nipp**ed at Sarah's overalls. She **fed** him an apple. Caleb and I stood behind Sarah.

"I can ride a horse, I know," said Sarah. "I rode once when I was twelve. I will ride Jack." Jack was Sarah's **favorite**.

Papa **shook** his head. "Not Jack," he said. "Jack is **sly**."

"I am sly, too," said Sarah **stubborn**ly.

Papa smiled. "Ayuh," he said, **nod**ding. "But not Jack."

"Yes, Jack!" Sarah's voice was very loud.

"I can teach you how to drive a wagon. I have already taught you how to **plow**."

"And then I can go to town. By myself."

"Say no, Papa," Caleb **whisper**ed beside me.

"That's a **fair** thing, Sarah," said Papa. "We'll **practice**."

A soft **rumble** of **thunder** sounded. Papa looked up at the clouds.

"Today? Can we begin today?" asked Sarah.

"Tomorrow is best," said Papa, looking worried. "I have to **fix** the house **roof**. A **portion** of it is **loose**. And there's a **storm** coming."

54

"We," said Sarah.

"What?" Papa turned.

"*We* will fix the roof," said Sarah. "I've done it before. I know about roofs. I am a good **carpenter**. Remember, I told you?"

There was thunder again, and Papa went to get the **ladder**.

"Are you fast?" he asked Sarah.

"I am fast and I am good," said Sarah. And they **climb**ed the ladder to the roof, Sarah with **wisps** of hair around her face, her mouth full of **nails**, overalls like Papa's. Overalls that *were* Papa's.

Caleb and I went inside to close the windows. We could hear the **steady** sound of **hammers pound**ing the roof **overhead**.

"Why does she want to go to town by herself?" asked Caleb. "To leave us?"

I shook my head, **weary** with Caleb's questions. Tears **gather**ed at the **corners** of my eyes. But there was no time to cry, for suddenly Papa **call**ed **out**.

"Caleb! Anna!"

We ran outside and saw a **huge** cloud, **horribly** black, moving toward us over the north fields. Papa **slid** down the roof, helping Sarah after him.

"A **squall!**" he **yell**ed to us. He held up his arms and Sarah jumped off the porch roof.

"Get the horses inside," he ordered Caleb. "Get the **sheep**, Anna. And the cows. The barn is safest."

The grasses **flatten**ed. There was a **hiss** of wind, a sudden **pungent** smell. Our faces looked yellow in the strange light. Caleb and I jumped over the fence and found the animals **huddle**d by the barn. I **count**ed the sheep to **make sure** they were all there, and **herd**ed them into a large **stall**. A few **raindrop**s came, **gentle** at first, then stronger and louder, so that Caleb and I **cover**ed our ears and **stare**d at each other without speaking. Caleb looked **frighten**ed and I tried to smile at him. Sarah carried a **sack** into the barn, her hair **wet** and **stream**ing down her neck, Papa came behind, Lottie and Nick with him, their ears **flat** against their heads.

"Wait!" cried Sarah. "My chickens!"

"No, Sarah!" Papa called after her. But Sarah had already run from the barn into a **sheet** of rain. My father **follow**ed her. The sheep **nose**d open their stall door and milled **around** the barn, **bleat**ing. Nick **crept** under my arm, and a **lamb**, Mattie with the black face, stood close to me, **trembling**. There was a soft **paw** on my **lap**, then a gray body. Seal. And then, as the thunder pounded and the wind rose and there was the **terrible crackling** of **lightning** close by, Sarah and Papa stood in the barn **doorway**, wet to the skin. Papa carried Sarah's chickens. Sarah came with an **armful** of summer roses.

Sarah's chickens were not afraid, and they **settled** like small red **bundle**s in the **hay**. Papa closed the door at last, shutting out some of the sounds of the storm. The barn was **eerie** and half lighted, like **dusk** without a **lantern**. Papa **spread blanket**s around our shoulders and Sarah **unpack**ed a bag of cheese and bread and jam. At the very bottom of the bag were Sarah's **shell**s.

Caleb got up and went over to the small barn window.

"What color is the sea when it storms?" he asked Sarah.

"Blue," said Sarah, **brush**ing her wet hair back with her fingers. "And gray and green."

Caleb nodded and smiled.

"Look," he said to her. "Look what is **missing** from

your **drawing**."

Sarah went to stand between Caleb and Papa by the window. She looked a long time without speaking. Finally, she touched Papa's shoulder.

"We have squalls in Maine, too," she said. "Just like this. It will be all right, Jacob."

Papa said nothing. But he put his arm around her, and leaned over to **rest** his **chin** in her hair. I closed my eyes, suddenly remembering Mama and Papa standing that way, Mama smaller than Sarah, her hair fair against Papa's shoulder. When I opened my eyes again, it was Sarah standing there. Caleb looked at me and smiled and smiled until he could smile no more.

We slept in the hay all night, waking when the wind was wild, sleeping again when it was quiet. And at **dawn** there was the sudden sound of **hail**, like stones **tossed** against the barn. We stared out the window, watching the ice **marbles bounce** on the ground. And when it was over we opened the barn door and walked out into the early-morning light. The hail **crunch**ed and **melt**ed **beneath** our feet. It was white and **gleam**ing for as far as we looked, like sun on glass. Like the sea.

9

It was very quiet. The dogs leaned down to eat the **hailstone**s. Seal stepped around them and **leap**ed up on the **fence** to **groom** herself. A tree had blown over near the cow **pond**. And the wild roses were **scatter**ed on the ground, as if a **wedding** had come and gone there. "I'm glad I saved an **armful**" was all that Sarah said.

Only one field was **badly damage**d, and Sarah and Papa **hitch**ed up the horses and **plowe**d and re**planted** during the next two days. The **roof** had held.

"I told you I know about roofs," Sarah told Papa, making him smile.

Papa **kept his promise** to Sarah. When the work was done, he took her out into the fields, Papa riding Jack who was **sly**, and Sarah riding Old Bess. Sarah was quick to learn.

"Too quick," Caleb **complain**ed to me as we watched from the fence. He thought a moment. "Maybe she'll **fall off** and have to stay here. Why?" he asked, turning to me. "Why does she have to go away **alone**?"

"**Hush** up, Caleb," I said **cross**ly. "Hush up."

"I could get sick and make her **stay** here," said Caleb.

"No."

"We could **tie** her up."

"No."

And Caleb began to cry, and I took him inside the **barn** where we could both cry.

Papa and Sarah came to hitch the horses to the **wagon**, so Sarah could **practice** driving. Papa didn't see Caleb's tears, and he sent him with an **ax** to begin **chop**ping up the tree by the pond for **firewood**. I stood and watched Sarah, the **reins** in her hands, Papa next to her in the wagon. I could see Caleb standing by the pond, one hand **shading** his eyes, watching, too. I went into the safe **darkness** of the barn then, Sarah's chickens **scuttling** along behind me.

"Why?" I asked out loud, **echo**ing Caleb's question.

The chickens watched me, their eyes small and bright.

The next morning Sarah got up early and put on her blue dress. She took apples to the barn. She **load**ed a **bundle** of **hay** on the wagon for Old Bess and Jack. She put on her yellow **bonnet**.

"Remember Jack," said Papa. "A strong hand."

"Yes, Jacob."

"Best to be home before dark," said Papa. "Driving a wagon is hard if there's no **full moon**."

"Yes, Jacob."

Sarah kissed us all, even my father, who looked surprised.

"Take care of Seal," she said to Caleb and me. And with a **whisper** to Old Bess and a **stern** word to Jack, Sarah **climb**ed up in the wagon and **drove away**.

"Very good," **murmur**ed Papa as he watched. And after a while he turned and went out into the fields.

Caleb and I watched Sarah from the porch. Caleb took my hand, and the dogs **lay** down beside us. It was sunny, and I remembered another time when a wagon had taken Mama away. It had been a day just like this day. And Mama had never come back.

Seal jumped up to the porch, her feet making a small **thump**. Caleb **lean**ed down and picked her up and walked inside. I took the **broom** and slowly **swept** the porch. Then I **water**ed Sarah's plants. Caleb cleaned out the wood **stove** and carried the **ashes** to the barn, **spill**ing them so that I had to sweep the porch again.

"I *am* loud and **pesky**," Caleb cried suddenly. "You said so! And she has gone to buy a train ticket to go away!"

"No, Caleb. She would tell us."

"The house is too small," said Caleb. "That's what it is."

"The house is not too small," I said.

I looked at Sarah's **drawing** of the fields **pinned** up on the wall next to the window.

"What is **missing**?" I asked Caleb. "You said you knew what was missing."

"Colors," said Caleb **wearily**. "The colors of the sea."

Outside, clouds moved into the sky and went away again. We took lunch to Papa, cheese and bread and lemonade. Caleb **nudged** me.

"Ask him. Ask Papa."

"What has Sarah gone to do?" I asked.

"I don't know," said Papa. He **squinted** at me. Then he **sighed** and put one hand on Caleb's head, one on mine. "Sarah is Sarah. She does things her way, you know."

"I know," said Caleb very softly.

Papa picked up his **shovel** and put on his hat.

"Ask if she's coming back," whispered Caleb.

"Of course she's coming back," I said. "Seal is here." But I would not ask the question. I was afraid to hear the answer.

We **fed** the **sheep**, and I set the table for dinner. Four plates. The sun dropped low over the west fields. Lottie and Nick stood at the door, **wagging** their tails, asking for **supper**. Papa came to light the stove. And then it was **dusk**. Soon it would be dark. Caleb sat on the **porch** steps, turning his moon **snail** shell **over and over** in his hand. Seal **brushed back and forth** against him.

Suddenly Lottie began to **bark**, and Nick jumped off the porch and ran down the road.

"**Dust!**" cried Caleb. He climbed the porch and stood

on the roof. "Dust, and a yellow bonnet!"

Slowly the wagon came around the **windmill** and the barn and the **windbreak** and into the yard, the dogs jumping happily beside it.

"Hush, dogs," said Sarah. And Nick **leap**ed up into the wagon to sit by Sarah.

Papa took the reins and Sarah climbed down from the wagon.

Caleb **burst** into tears.

"Seal was very worried!" he cried.

Sarah put her arms around him, and he **wail**ed into her dress. "And the house is too small, we thought! And I am loud and pesky!"

Sarah looked at Papa and me over Caleb's head.

"We thought you might be thinking of leaving us," I told her. "Because you miss the sea."

Sarah smiled.

"No," she said. "I will always miss my old home, but the **truth** of it is I would miss you more."

Papa smiled at Sarah, then he **bent** quickly to **unhitch** the horses from the wagon. He led them to the barn for water.

Sarah **hand**ed me a **package**.

"For Anna," she said. "And Caleb. For all of us."

The package was small, **wrap**ped in brown paper with a **rubber** band around it. Very carefully I **unwrap**ped it, Caleb **peer**ing closely. Inside were three colored pencils.

"Blue," said Caleb slowly, "and gray. And green."

Sarah **nod**ded.

Suddenly Caleb **grin**ned.

"Papa," he called. "Papa, come quickly! Sarah has brought the sea!"

*We eat our night meal by **candlelight**, the four of us. Sarah has brought candles from town. And nasturtium **seed**s for her garden, and a book of songs to teach us. It is late, and Caleb is nearly sleeping by his plate and Sarah is smiling at my father. Soon there will be a wedding. Papa says that when the **preacher** asks if he will have Sarah for his wife, he will answer, "Ayuh."*

Autumn *will come, then winter, cold with a wind that **blow**s like the wind off the sea in Maine. There will be **nest**s of **curl**s to look for, and **dried** flowers all winter long. When there are **storm**s, Papa will **stretch** a **rope** from the door to the barn so we will not be **lost** when we feed the sheep and the cows and Jack and Old Bass. And Sarah's* chickens, if they aren't living in the house. There will be Sarah's sea, blue and gray and green, **bang**ing on the wall. And songs, old ones and new. And Seal with yellow eyes. And there will be Sarah, **plain** and tall.